AF228190

AMAZING ART FORMS

The Art of Film

BY MARY SHAW

Kids Core

An Imprint of Abdo Publishing
abdobooks.com

abdobooks.com

Published by Abdo Publishing, a division of ABDO, PO Box 398166, Minneapolis, Minnesota 55439. Copyright © 2025 by Abdo Consulting Group, Inc. International copyrights reserved in all countries. No part of this book may be reproduced in any form without written permission from the publisher. Kids Core™ is a trademark and logo of Abdo Publishing.

Printed in the United States of America, North Mankato, Minnesota.
102024
012025

Cover Photo: Shutterstock Images
Interior Photo: Andriy Shevchuk/Shutterstock Images, 4–5; Shutterstock Images, 6, 7, 12–13, 14, 16, 29 (top); Lebrecht Music & Arts/Alamy, 9; Eric Broder Van Dyke/Shutterstock Images, 10; Valentine Chapuis/AFP/Getty Images, 18; Sean Pavone/Shutterstock Images, 20–21; Michael Tran/FilmMagic/Getty Images, 23; Mike Marsland/WireImage/Getty Images, 24; Red Line Editorial, 25; John Shearer/WireImage/Getty Images, 26; SDI Productions/iStockphoto, 28 (top); Lauren Elisabeth/Shutterstock Images, 28 (bottom); DC Studio/Shutterstock Images, 29 (bottom)

Editor: Haley Williams
Series Designer: Katharine Hale

Library of Congress Control Number: 2024938348

Publisher's Cataloging-in-Publication Data

Names: Shaw, Mary, author.
Title: The art of film / by Mary Shaw
Description: Minneapolis, Minnesota: ABDO Publishing, 2025 | Series: Amazing art forms | Includes online resources and index.
Identifiers: ISBN 9781098295769 (lib. bdg.) | ISBN 9798384916765 (ebook)
Subjects: LCSH: Art--Juvenile literature. | Motion picture film--Juvenile literature. | Film industry (Motion pictures)--Juvenile literature. | Features (Motion pictures)--Juvenile literature. | Art--Technique--Juvenile literature. | Arts and history--Juvenile literature.
Classification: DDC 791.43--dc23

CONTENTS

People can use a smartphone or a video camera to record films.

CHAPTER 1

Lights, Camera, Action!

"Cut!" yelled Mack. Mack was directing his first film. It was about an astronaut finding an alien. His friends were helping him with the film. Levi and Olivia were the actors. Jacky made the **props**. And Rose made the costumes.

A clapperboard, or film slate, is a board that tells people what scene is being shot.

Mack was the film's **cinematographer**. He captured the story that was being told and made sure the camera was recording the actors. Mack was also the director. This meant he helped guide the actors during the **scenes**. He would tell them if they were too far away from the camera. He would also let them know if they needed to talk louder.

Once they were finished filming, Mack's friend Lydia would **edit** the film on

Many parks around the world host outdoor movie nights where large groups of people can watch films together.

her computer. Then Mack and his friends could plan the film's premiere! But first, they had to film the next scene. Levi and Olivia took their places. Mack hit record on his video camera. Then he yelled, "Action!"

What Is Film?

Film is the art form of capturing moving pictures. These pictures are put together to create a story. Films are also known as movies or motion pictures. A person who creates films is called a filmmaker.

The first motion picture was created in 1878. It was a series of photographs that were

Nickelodeons

The first indoor movie theaters were called nickelodeons. These theaters were popular in big cities during the early 1900s. The name for these movie theaters combined the Greek word for theater, *odeon*, with the cost of a ticket. For one nickel, moviegoers could watch short films in an indoor theater.

British photographer Eadweard Muybridge created the first motion picture. It is called *The Horse in Motion.*

projected to make a horse look as if it were moving. People were fascinated by the new art form.

Early films did not have sound. Instead, movie theaters hired people to play live music during the film. The first movie with sound released in 1927. It is called *The Jazz Singer.*

Movie theaters often have posters showing new, popular, and upcoming films.

Early movies were in black and white. Adding color to films became popular in the late 1930s. Movies such as *The Wizard of Oz* used bright and exciting colors that people had not seen on screen before.

Films have changed a lot over time. Today, most films use color and sound. Some are still created by recording actors using a video camera. Others are made entirely on computers. No matter how they are made, movies are enjoyed by people around the world.

Movies may be shot at a real location or in a studio. For studio filming, sets must be built to create the scenes.

12

How Movies Are Made

There are many steps involved in creating a movie. All movies begin in pre-production. This is the planning stage. Producers are a big part of the creation of a movie. They come up with ideas for a story. Producers hire writers to complete the **script**.

Writers help create stories and characters. They also decide what characters will say and do.

Artists create a storyboard. A storyboard is used to show what the movie will look like. It is like a first draft. Artists draw the scenes of a movie in boxes called panels. Panels describe the actions in the movie from beginning to end. The panels may include **dialogue**. The storyboard also shows where the camera will shoot from and what will be filmed.

The next step is putting together a crew. This includes jobs such as makeup artists and costume designers. Actors audition to play roles or voice characters. Once the actors and crew are selected, it is time to begin filming.

Film Styles

There are many styles of film. Live action is when real actors play characters. Animated movies use a computer to create characters and scenes. Voice actors read the lines for the characters. Movies such as *Star Wars* and *Jurassic Park* use a mix of film styles. Some parts are live action. Others are created using computers.

A take is a single shooting of a scene. Simple scenes may have one or two takes while more complex scenes can have hundreds of takes.

Production

Production is when the filming process begins. During this stage, scenes are often shot out of order. This is done to save time and money.

During filming, the director helps the actors with their performances. The director also instructs the crew on how a scene should be filmed.

There are many important roles in the production process. A boom operator makes sure the sound is properly recorded. Camera operators record the actors using video cameras. A gaffer is the person in charge of lighting a set.

Post-Production

Once the video and audio are recorded, post-production begins. This is the stage when all the elements of a film are put together. Many people work together to create the final movie. Editors put scenes into the correct order.

Animated and computer-generated movies can take several years to create, depending on the length of the film and the amount of detail that is added.

They use the storyboard as a guide. If a movie is too long, some scenes are cut or shortened.

Sound engineers add or take out sounds from the movie. Background music may also be added. If the movie needs special effects, visual effects artists will add in computer generated imagery (CGI).

Once a film has gone through a few rounds of editing, the final cut is ready. This is the version of the movie that audiences will watch. Film studios send the final cut to movie theaters. Then audiences can enjoy the film!

Explore Online

Visit the website below. Does it give any new information about how movies are made that wasn't in Chapter Two?

How Are Movies Made?

abdocorelibrary.com/art-of-film

Hollywood Boulevard features many famous film-related tourist attractions, including movie theaters, museums, and the Hollywood Walk of Fame.

Places and People in Film

Movies are made all over the world. Many movies are created in Hollywood, California. India also has a large movie industry. The biggest producer of Indian films is Bollywood. These films often use song and dance to tell stories.

Famous Filmmakers

There are many famous filmmakers around the world. Hayao Miyazaki is a Japanese animator and director. He founded an animation studio called Studio Ghibli in 1985. Many of Miyazaki's movies explore fantasy worlds. One of his most famous animated films is *Spirited Away*.

Director Steven Spielberg is an American filmmaker. He has made several popular

Bollywood

Bollywood was created in Mumbai, India, in the 1930s. It produces between 1,500 and 2,000 movies a year. That is more movies than what Hollywood releases each year. Today, many Bollywood films are released around the world in 20 different languages.

In 2023, Hayao Miyazaki released his twelfth film, *The Boy and the Heron.* He both wrote and directed the film.

movies, including *E. T. the Extra-Terrestrial* and *Jurassic Park.* Tim Burton is a director and producer. He often creates dark and creepy films. One of his most popular movies is the animated film *Coraline.*

Director Ava DuVernay's films often focus on the experiences of Black Americans. DuVernay has received many awards for her work. The movie *Selma* is one of her most well-known films.

Along with being a director, Greta Gerwig is also an actor and writer.

Greta Gerwig is another famous filmmaker. She directed *Barbie*. She was the first woman to direct a movie that made more than $1 billion in ticket sales.

Film Festivals and Awards

There are several film festivals held each year to celebrate new movies. One of the biggest is the Toronto International Film Festival. It is held every year in Toronto, Canada. Another famous

Top Five Highest-Earning Movies

Movie	Director(s)	Year Released	Earnings
Avatar	James Cameron	2009	$2.92 billion
Avengers: Endgame	Anthony Russo and Joe Russo	2019	$2.79 billion
Avatar: The Way of Water	James Cameron	2022	$2.32 billion
Titanic	James Cameron	1997	$2.26 billion
Star Wars: Episode VII– The Force Awakens	J. J. Abrams	2015	$2.07 billion

This chart shows the top five highest-earning films in the world through July 2024. The earnings come from the time each film spent in theaters, including the release and re-releases.

festival is the Sundance Film Festival in Utah.

The Tribeca Film Festival is also popular. It takes

place in New York.

The Academy Awards, also known as the Oscars, is one of the biggest film award ceremonies. The Oscars celebrates the world's best films and actors. The Golden Globe Awards ceremony is another important event. These awards honor the best films, television shows, and actors from around the world.

Films tell stories with moving pictures. They create new worlds for audiences to explore. Film is an art form that brings people together.

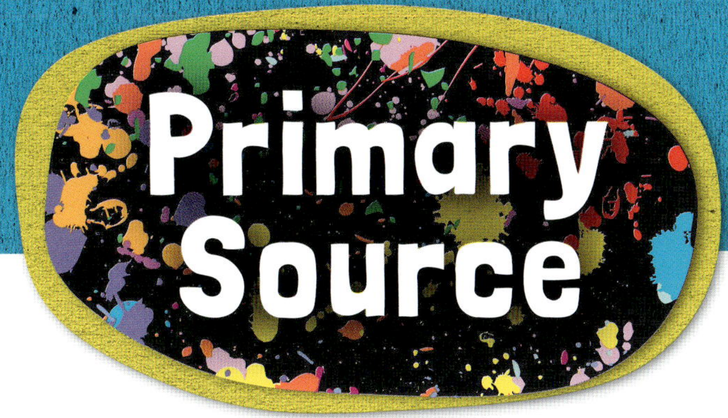

In 2023, Greta Gerwig talked about her experience working on the movie *Barbie* and what it is like to be a director:

> As a director, you have the job of dreaming up the movie, and then you have to get everyone else in the movie—*hundreds* of people—to have that same dream, too.

Source: Alex Moshakis. "'It Had to Be Totally Bananas': Greta Gerwig on Bringing Barbie to Life." *Guardian*, 9 July 2023, theguardian.com. Accessed 6 May 2024.

What's the Big Idea?

Read this quote carefully. What is its main idea? Explain how the main idea is supported by details.

Art Supplies

Script

Costumes and makeup

Video camera, lights, and microphone

Computer for editing

Glossary

cinematographer

a person who directs the camera crew on a film set

dialogue

a conversation between two or more people in a movie, script, or book

edit

to correct, cut, add to, or change with the goal of producing a finished piece of writing or a film

projected

displayed as an image or video, often by shining light onto a surface

props

objects that actors can interact with in a film

scene

a section of a film, play, or video

script

a written guide for a film or show that includes actors' lines

Online Resources

To learn more about film, visit our free resource websites below.

Visit **abdocorelibrary.com** or scan this QR code for free Common Core resources for teachers and students, including vetted activities, multimedia, and booklinks, for deeper subject comprehension.

Visit **abdobooklinks.com** or scan this QR code for free additional online weblinks for further learning. These links are routinely monitored and updated to provide the most current information available.

Learn More

Abdo, Kenny. *The Making of Star Wars*. Abdo, 2024.

Barretta, Gene. *Starring Steven Spielberg*. Little, Brown and Company, 2022.

O'Meara, Mallory. *Girls Make Movies*. Running Kids, 2023.

Index

About the Author

Mary Shaw is an editor, designer, and writer of children's books. She lives in Minneapolis, Minnesota. She used to make movies with her friends as a kid and is a regular at her local movie theater.